Watch me grow

Puppy

LONDON, NEW YORK, MUNICH,
MELBOURNE, and DELHI

Written and edited by Lisa Magloff
Design and digital artwork by Sonia Moore
DTP designer Almudena Díaz
Picture researcher Sarah Pownall
Production Emma Hughes

Jacket Design Hedi Gutt

Publishing manager Sue Leonard
Managing art editor Clare Shedden

First American Edition, 2005

Published in the United States by
DK Publishing, Inc.
375 Hudson Street
New York, NY 10014

05 06 07 08 09 10 9 8 7 6 5 4 3 2 1

A Cataloging-in-Publication record for this book
is available from the Library of Congress.

ISBN 0-7566-1273-X

Color reproduction by Coloursystems
Printed and bound in China by South China Printing Co. Ltd

Discover more at
www.dk.com

Contents

I am a dog

I have a wet, black nose and a long pink tongue. I love to play and chase after things. My long tail swishes back and forth when I am happy or excited.

The fur has a thick undercoat and a fine outer coat.

Labrador retriever
Retriever dogs are trained to grab things in their mouths and bring them back. They also love to run and chase things.

Snore, snore... lots of puppies, all snuggled up to sleep.

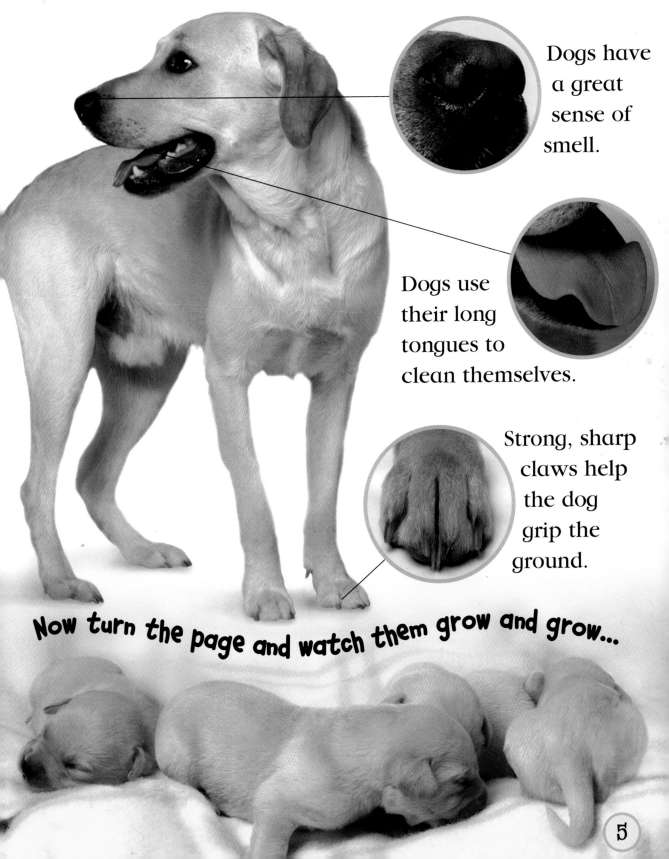

Dogs have a great sense of smell.

Dogs use their long tongues to clean themselves.

Strong, sharp claws help the dog grip the ground.

Now turn the page and watch them grow and grow...

My mom and dad

My mom and dad live on a farm. They like to run and play together. But after my brothers and sisters and I are born, Mom will take care of us by herself.

This is my mom.

Mom's tummy.

Can you see how big the mother dog's tummy is? The puppies have been growing inside her for eight weeks. Soon they will be born.

This is my dad.

Dog facts

🐕 Dogs sweat through the cushioned pads of their feet.

🐕 A dogs' sense of smell is so good that a dog can smell each ingredient in a pot of stew.

🐕 Dogs can see well in the dark. They can see some colors, but probably not red or green.

🐕 Dogs bark to tell other dogs that something is happening.

After a bath, Dad likes to shake himself dry!

We are three days old

Mom gave birth to us in a warm, safe place. We can't see or hear, but we can smell and wriggle around. We spend most of our time eating, sleeping, and staying warm and cozy.

The puppies nurse by gently pushing Mom's nipples with their paws.

It's a tight squeeze

The puppies squirm and shove to find a nipple and begin drinking their mother's milk. They will nurse every three or four hours.

No pushing, there's room for everyone.

Now we can see

Our eyes opened when we were nine days old. Now we are learning to walk. Mom wants us to stay close to her, but we're curious about the world and want to explore.

The puppies still spend most of their time sleeping.

Learning to walk

The puppies are still unsteady on their feet, but they will soon be strong enough to run and play.

Growing up is hard work!

It's time to explore

I'm six weeks old and big enough to explore the house on my own. There are so many interesting things to see! It's fun finding new toys to play with.

Learning by playing
The puppies have sharp teeth now, and they chew and play with everything.

Puppies say "hello" to new friends by sniffing them.

Sniff sniff... come on, bear, let's play!

Dinner time

The puppies can eat solid food. They are still nursing, but they nurse less each day. Soon they will be weaned and eat only solid food.

I'm three months old

It's time for me to start exploring the forest. With my long muzzle I can smell all the insects and plants in the woods.

This puppy has found an exciting smell, buried deep in the leaves.

On the scent

Dogs have a much better sense of smell than people. Dogs use smell to find food and as a way to recognize other dogs and humans.

Playing with Dad

I am six months old and now I am almost as big as Dad. When I play tug-of-war with Dad, he growls to let me know that he is still in charge of our family.

Come on, Dad! Let me have the stick!

Dogs of all ages learn and grow by playing games.

Super swimmers

Most dogs are very good swimmers, but some like the water better than others. All dogs use the same swimming stroke— the dog paddle.

Grrrr...

I'm one year old

While I've been busy growing up, our family has grown bigger. Mom and Dad have had six new puppies. These are my new brothers and sisters.

My cousin

My aunt

Here I am

My dad

Many dogs enjoy living in a big, friendly family group like this one.

My mom

Busy mom
Adult female dogs can have two litters of puppies each year, starting when they are just six months old.

The circle of life goes around and around

Now you know how I turned into a grown-up dog.

My friends from around the world

My doggy friends from around the world have many jobs to do, so they come in lots of sizes and shapes.

The Kerry Blue terrier comes from Ireland and loves the water.

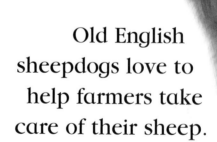

Old English sheepdogs love to help farmers take care of their sheep.

Bassett hounds come from France, where they were once used as hunting dogs.

The Chihuahua comes from Mexico and is the world's smallest dog.

Afghan hounds have been used as hunting dogs for thousands of years.

woof, woof—I help move sheep around the farm.

This Pomeranian is 1ft (30 cm) tall.

Doggy facts
....

Dogs can hear many sounds that humans cannot, such as insects flying.

The first animal in space was a Russian dog named Laika, in 1957.

Glossary

Retrieve
To find something and bring it back. Labradors are good retrievers.

Growl
A warning noise that tells other dogs or people to watch out.

Nurse
When a baby animal, such as a puppy, drinks its mother's milk.

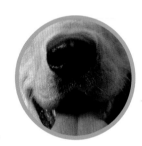
Muzzle
The name for the nose and mouth of some animals, including dogs.

Fur
The soft hair on a dog that keeps it warm and protects it.

Wean
When a baby stops drinking milk and starts to eat solid food.

Acknowledgments
The publisher would like to thank the following for their kind permission to reproduce their photographs:
Key: t = top, b = bottom, l = left, r = right, bkgrd = background, c = center

4 Alamy Images: Stefanie Krause-Wieczorek cl. 7 Corbis: Tom Stewart br. 19 Science Photo Library: Reneé Lynn tr. 24 Ridgeway Labradors: br. All other pictures © Dorling Kindersley Media Library.

For further information see: www.dkimages.com

Watch Me Grow Puppy would not have been possible to make without the assistance of Ridgeway Labradors in Oxfordshire, England. We would particularly like to thank Helen and Stephen Harvey for their time and patience while loaning us their house, grounds, and dogs. Thanks also to our canine friends Chloe, Phoebe, Timmy, TJ, Harvey, and Roxy.